Self-Control

Julie Murray

Abdo Kids Junior
is an Imprint of Abdo Kids
abdobooks.com

Abdo
CHARACTER EDUCATION
Kids

abdobooks.com

Published by Abdo Kids, a division of ABDO, P.O. Box 398166, Minneapolis, Minnesota 55439.

Printed in the United States of America, North Mankato, Minnesota.

102019

012020

Photo Credits: iStock, Shutterstock

Production Contributors: Teddy Borth, Jennie Forsberg, Grace Hansen

Design Contributors: Christina Doffing, Candice Keimig, Dorothy Toth

Library of Congress Control Number: 2019941199

Publisher's Cataloging-in-Publication Data

Names: Murray, Julie, author.

Title: Self-Control / by Julie Murray

Description: Minneapolis, Minnesota : Abdo Kids, 2020 | Series: Character education | Includes online resources and index.

Identifiers: ISBN 9781532188695 (lib. bdg.) | ISBN 9781644942772 (pbk.) | ISBN 9781532189180 (ebook) | ISBN 9781098200169 (Read-to-Me ebook)

Subjects: LCSH: Self-control--Juvenile literature. | Self-discipline--Juvenile literature. | Feelings--Juvenile literature. | Moral ideas--Juvenile literature.

Classification: DDC 152.4--dc23

Table of Contents

Self-Control

Having self-control can be hard.

It is **controlling** what you do and how you feel.

It's **Halloween**. Leo wants lots of candy. But he only takes one piece.

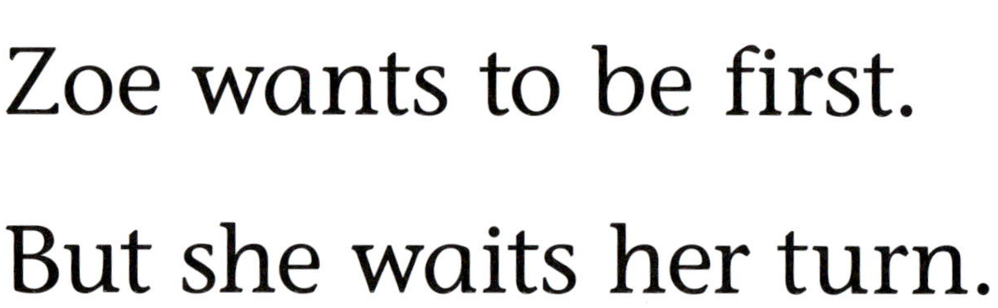

Zoe wants to be first.

But she waits her turn.

Eva wants the toy. She wants to scream. But she puts it back on the shelf.

Brad is mad. He wants to hit Alex. But he walks away.

It's time to go. Ike wants to keep playing. But he walks home with his mom.

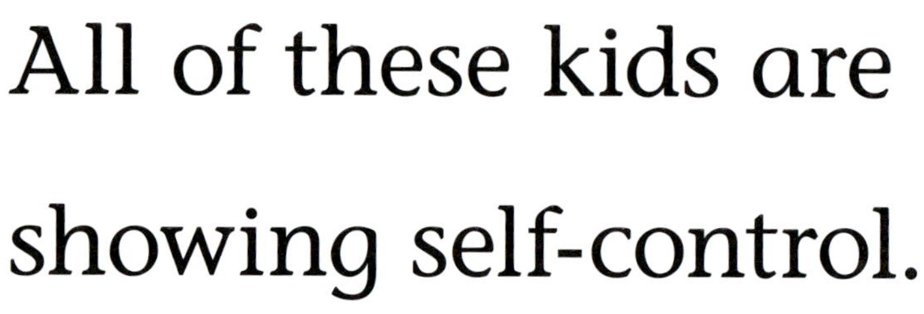
All of these kids are showing self-control.

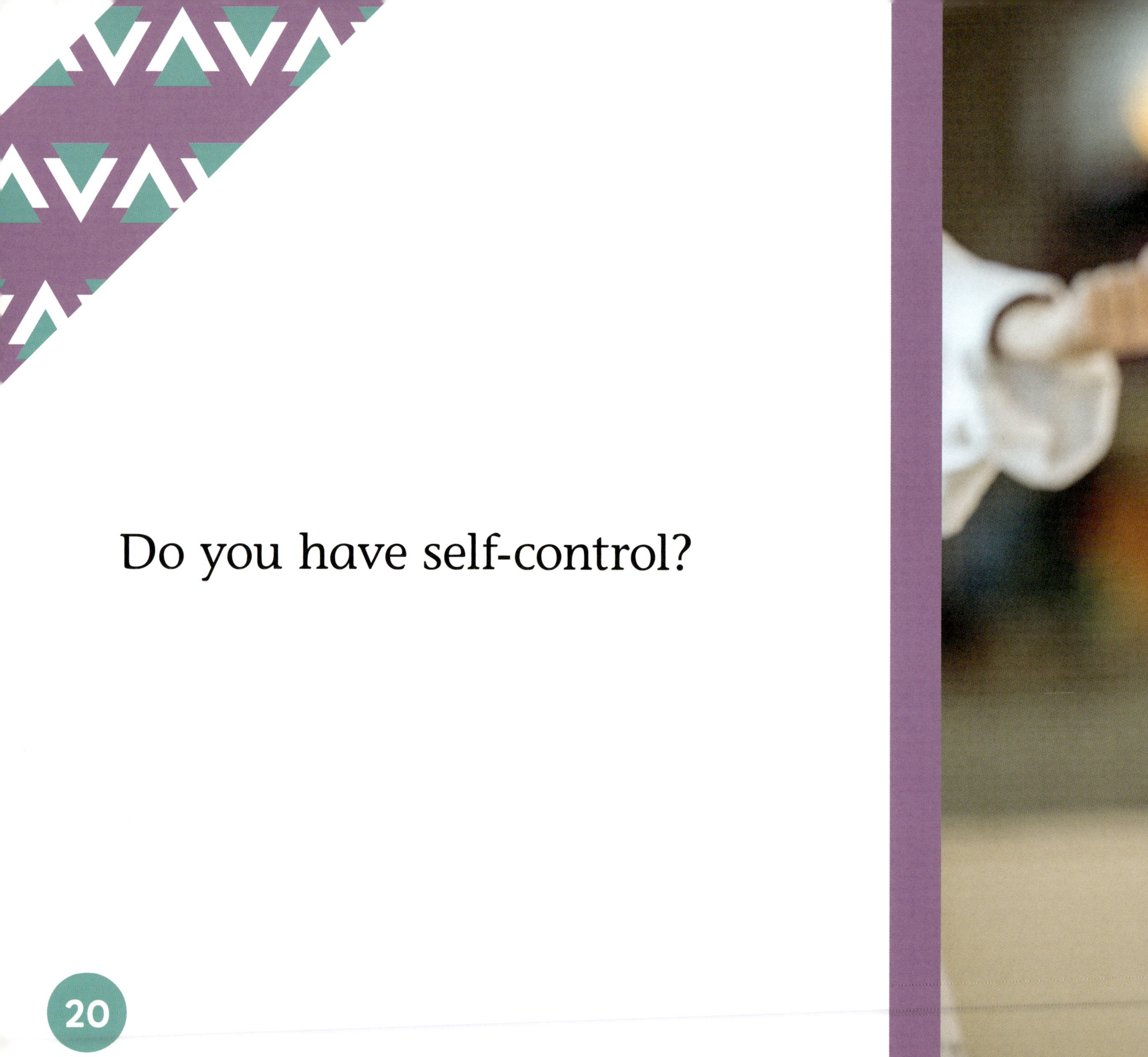

Do you have self-control?

Ways to Have Self-Control

count to 5

take a deep breath

think of ways to make it better

walk away

Glossary

controlling
holding back or showing restraint.

Halloween
a holiday celebrated on October 31st where people dress in costume and trick-or-treat.

Index

Visit **abdokids.com** to access crafts, games, videos, and more!

Use Abdo Kids code

CSK8695

or scan this QR code!